CU00418363

On the Night Tide

ON THE NIGHT TIDE

David Hodges

Br David

On the Night Tide
© David Hodges 2001

ISBN 0 9533222 38

Acknowledgements
Spirituality and *The Tablet*
in which some of these poems first appeared

Published by The Abbey, Caldey Island,
Tenby, Pembs. SA70 7UH, Wales, GB.

On the Night Tide

On the Night Tide

As we cut across
rays of dancing light,
drumming engine
above the water sound,
soon the harbour lights
become a distant ring
beyond the black
and seaspray.

Thoughts drift
between
regret and expectation,
seeking a glimpse
of the far shore,
but soon
the sea fills
all my thoughts.

The Buck

I came upon him
trespassing
from the wild,
the sun just risen,
the cornfields shimmering,
white-topped,
the horizon still and clear.
Wanting to investigate,
he is shy,
his ears flapping
with fear;
delicate, light-footed,
he bounds away.
Can he live
without the wild?
He has his landscape;
I have mine.

That night, a speeding car,
a crunch of brakes,
finds him lying in the ditch,
rigid with fear;
his watchful eyes
shining,
responding, as I trace
the silhouette of his face,
calming his fear.
Unharmed, recovering
the safety of his trees,
he turns, looks back,
then bounds away.
Can he live
without the wild?
He has his landscape;
I have mine.

Sunrise below Sulham Wood

That moment caught
of perfect beauty.
Two does, watchful,
grouping on the rise,
below the black of trees;
the young buck
leaping, bounding,
along the line of mist.
Moment of awe and innocence;
the earth awakening,
the red sun
creeping.

"We are the bees of the invisible..."

Rilke, letter to Witold von Hulewicz

"We've never, no, not for a single day,
pure space before us, such as that which flowers
endlessly open into..."
Rilke, Duino Elegies VIII

The glory of the rose
revealed in time,
minute perfection,
born from a freedom
limited yet pure;
while we, with our
so celebrated liberty,
cry freedom, yet find
ways ever more complex
to restrain the other,
out of step
with creation's healing touch,
made for the invisible
yet, despite our longing,
clinging
ever more tenaciously
to the visible.

With our divided minds
distracted by the past and future,
unable to abandon
to the eternal present,
out of tune
with nature's rhythm,
yet we must find
that undisturbed space
at the centre of the rose.

For our task is God-given,
like Rilke's bees
to transform the visible
into the invisible,
the growth of love beyond desire;
the poet's task
to glimpse the eternal
behind the flux of time,
living in two worlds
until both
become one.

Pilgrimage

Sharing space
in the wild
with a gnarled
black walnut tree,
born out of the landscape,
in the endless
empty plain.
I am glad
of its deep shade
and of the water-hole
shimmering
beneath the burning heat,
where dreams surface,
self is encountered,
and illusions shattered;
where wounds are healed,
and reality faced;
where God is tasted,
in the slow
march of time,
on the path of longing,
towards that holy place
we travel to.

Returning to Caldey

Through "the Scares"*,
across the bow
the land takes shape,
tops of trees
dipped in sunlight,
cliffs stark in shadow,
birds in flight
tracing the shoreline;
the lapping water
in tune
with that silent melody
sending shivers to my heart.

*A sea passage between rock and cliff
giving first sight of Caldey Island

Seals

Seals basking
on a narrow ledge,
shuffling, jostling,
flippers flapping,
playfully slapping.
One flopping
into water,
others joining
loudly splashing,
noses poking,
heads bobbing,
sleek backs
shining, diving,
reappearing
gulping air,
whiskers dripping,
curious eyes
watching.

In flight. In flight

Seabird
pure as starlight,
flashing fast across
a bay of brilliant blue,
skimming, dipping
on the sea's swell,
snow-white feathers
merging with the sea-spray.

Pitting wits
against wind and sea,
tacking
against a gusting breeze;
later, by the cliff edge
floating on the updraughts.
Soaring, circling high above,
wings like shining silver;
dropping
into a dive, pulling out,
wingtip to wingtip
shimmering in the sunlight.

Hours pass,
brighter and brighter,
lost in wonder:
seabird in free flight,
underbelly
now pink
in the sunset.

Nothing in November

Nothing in November
but dark days
of black seas raging,
pounding the broken shore,
blinding spray
and the foam roaring,
pouring
through the red teeth
of the red raw rock,
scarred by the buffeting
of endless storms
and the wild sea lashing.
Dark days merge into nights
when the sea of my heart
refuses rest.

When the biting cold
chills the bone,
and the endless
roar and motion,
and the cry
of the storm-tossed gulls
singing, ringing in the air;
when the howl
of the salt-laden wind,
sharp as a knife,
cuts into the soul,
until the unbearable
endless night
meets the dawn...
and the gentle rain.

Night Tide

Ebb and flow
Ebb and flow
Eternal rhythm
Rhythm of the universe
Continual going and returning
Creation's ceaseless recreation
New life rising from decay

Love destroying hate
Unity from division
Self-love becomes self-giving
Trust replaces fear
Escape becomes surrender
into love
Giving and receiving
Returning love for love
Returning love
to the source of love

Ebb and flow
Ebb and flow
All being responding
Symbol of eternal longing
Eternal Father begetting Son
All creation giving birth
Maternal Spirit conceiving

The Playfulness of God

Out of a milky sea,
huge white-topped rollers
poised to crash,
pounding against red rock,
the foam pushed high,
hung in suspense
like a freeze-frame,
floating on air, then
pouring up ragged cliffs,
spume flecking,
driven by a wild wind
across undulating fields
of bent grass.

A flock of starlings,
together rising,
cheeky stunt fliers
challenging the gusting wind,
all in formation,
then circling and pirouetting,
disappearing, reappearing,
a trick of the light,
an aerial ballet, then
playfully tossing like acrobats
over a drystone wall,
scattering on the meadow
like fallen leaves.

In the playfulness of God,
all is now and wonder.

Birds Migrating South

That unearthly silence,
that moment suspended in time,
before they rise
with the flutter of many wings
and muffled cries,
circle, peel off, loop and cross,
join,
divide again.
Birds in formation,
nearer, further,
nearer, further,
as they pass
and repass overhead;
suddenly
veering south,
the sight
and the sound
of a thousand
beating wings
flying seaward,
silver in the sun.

Rock Pool

Tranquil,
seaweed-sided,
tidal pool
with green and red
and purple fronds;
tiny fish,
black and silver,
darting in the sunlight;
microcosm
of the roaring,
rolling, sea.

Absorbed
in a world
in miniature,
the mind relaxes,
worries disappear.
The rock pool,
its lazy calm,
a mirror
of the conscious mind;
the unconscious,
the thundering deep
behind.

The Orchard

The joy of
spring blossom
and the gentle breeze
on my face
and through my hair.
Nothing but birdsong
and the splash
of the stream
in the late afternoon,
filling the quiet
of the orchard
where I lie
in the long grass,
listening to the trees
and the wind moving gently,
enjoying the solitude
of silent thoughts,
content to wait
for the day's end
under the cool clear sky.

A Monk's Cell

A simple cell
a desk, a chair
a bed, a wooden cross
a life pared down to zero

The sacred text
a single thought
a silent prayer
a life raised up

Roof Conversion

They're re-roofing the Abbey,
keeping the shell,
stripping away,
repairing where it's rotted,
stopping the leaks,
filling in the cracks,
trying to restore
to the image of the original.

They've erected the scaffold,
we're hung in suspense,
they've uncovered and shamed us,
exposed us
to the elements;
but we're remaining in situ
to await the transformation,
suffering the tumult,
almost feeling the blows,
and the sound of the banging,
and the thumping and thudding,
of hammers
as they nail on the cross
battens,
while we pray the psalms.

The Old Priory

What mysteries
lie hidden here?
Leaning spire, grey stone walls,
tower, pond and rushes;
heavy doors and cobbled floors,
stone steps spiral
to a loft and tower above;
below, the choir,
the chant now silent;
sanctuary with its barrelled ceiling;
Ogham stone with its Cross
and ancient script;
old gatehouse, dovecote,
cloister, kitchen with its oven,
monks' living quarters
with battlements above;
an ancient well,
stepped ponds,
walled gardens in the valley;
the old mill
with its broken stone,
beds of cress
and running stream.

What history it tells
of holy monks,
Samson, Illtud, Dyfrig,
David, Gildas, Paul of Leon;
of pirates, pilgrims,
Viking raiders,
and lesser men now dead.
Why does the Black Monk
still make his lonely passage
in the night?
And that well, was Pyro
really drunk,
and did he drown there?

18

Where was that monk bricked up
with the Glastonbury jewels?
Does Paul Jones lie buried
in the bay?
And is there treasure sunk?
What else lies buried deep?
What other secrets
does the Priory keep?

Dawn at Sénanque*

On the Plateau de Vaucluse
where fragrant fields
of lavender,
deep, undulating furrows
of spiky purple blossoms,
stretch for miles
to distant bare mountains
shining like amethyst,
in the morning sun
under an azure sky.

In a rift in the plateau,
sitting snugly in the valley,
stark,
with the early morning sun
playing on white stone walls
and brown stone roofs,
lies the Abbey,
framed in lavender,
with its Roman bell-tower
and circular apse.

In the ethereal glow
of early morning light,
flooding through
the transept window,
monks descend the night stairs
to the sound of bells for Lauds.
A celebration of light and line,
and the ancient chant of psalms,
meet the Lord in his creation
to the praise of God on high.

*Cistercian Abbey of the Common Observance in Provence

Winter in Brown Candover

You found me on a ridge,
searching a distant line
of poplars,
bare, leafless, stubborn black,
against the grey of the world's end,
across acres of sodden, furrowed earth.

I had forgotten the silver sun
would come again.

Poem for a Blind Man

Sun and sudden shadow
on myriad greens,
sunburned fields
and scattered poppies,
all excite my senses;
but I cannot distil its message
or capture it in words
for winter evenings.

Such words have no message
for my blind friend,
on the sun porch
in his cane chair,
with the sun
and the breeze
on his young skin.
He hears the rustle
of the wind
through grass and tree
and knows a hundred birds
by a hundred calls,
a symphony
trapped and echoing
in the ring of trees.
He has not seen
but his mind holds
its mystery.

I long to show him
butterflies floating
in the sun,
bright insects dancing
in the cool shade
of the brook.
But already he sees
more than I see.

I take him with me
and we walk through
acres of tall grass;
I bring him home
and ask him
how it feels.

Poem for a Blind Man (2)

In my despair I cried out,
wondered why the blind man rejoiced
when all I saw was darkness.
Then he came to me and whispered,
turned me round to face the breeze,
raised his arms
and caught
handfuls of wind.

Sunset at Wherwell

Quiet, peaceful, grey on green
and running river;
purple-tinted leaves
on shadowed trees;
pale-flecked yellow haze
from now between the clouds;
and distant merging bands
of blue and orange;
reflection of a heron's shadow
on the gold-licked water;
and now the gentle breeze
through reed and grass.

The sun moves out of shelter;
then all transfixed and watching,
as it finds the ash tree,
adds a rose tint to the grey,
a faint smile to the valley,
and then is gone,
taking all its sleepy colours with it;
leaving only dusky outlines,
the breeze
and the shivering grass about my feet.

An awed silence,
when all but the moorhen
shy from rivalling the day's end.

Scintilla of Time

From my window, pink blossoms
against the cold, grey sky beyond.
Birds in formation
appear from the far distance,
the pattern constantly changing,
between fragrant pink blossoms.

Remembering Other Times

The night is cool and still,
the carved stone glistening
after gentle rain.
Looking up,
I cannot see our star;
spring blossom in the moonlight
now brings sadness to my heart.
Remembering other times,
I go to the lychgate alone.

Seeing Salvation

Do we recognise the Christ
who comes before us suffering
daily in the hungry,
tortured and oppressed?
Do we see
on that dread Cross
those we are complicit
in the murder of?
Do we prefer perhaps to sublimate
for reality, in viewing
sanitised objects
of devotion?
Not so challenging
as footage of the passion
suffered daily
in victims of our warfare
and oppression;
yes, of the wars we profit from
by weapons sales,
or in countries we've abandoned
when the profit in it fell;
or the wars we allow
to give ourselves a little peace;
or the scapegoats
that ease the pressure
on the politicians back at home
and boost their flagging ratings
– after all the real thing's
better than the movies.

Do we see Christ
in the face of one more child
that lost his childhood
to give us more cheap imports,
or in the maimed
and the oppressed,
in Asian factories and sweatshops;

or in the cheated peasants
on their mortgaged farms,
working to repay
a debt that will never be repaid?
But Christ redeemed us free,
wiped out all our debt,
took all our sin and shame.
Yes, Christ is in there where the hurt is.
But do we even love Him in our neighbour,
we who profess to love Him
in our enemy?

Up to our necks in structural sin.

Surfing the Net

They're assembling
a virtual world,
rewiring the globe.
It's an interactive
world now,
a borderless world
connected,
a sleepless world
in 24/7.
It's a multi-media
future
in cyberspace
but, excuse me,
where do the poor
fit in?
Where are the flood victims
when the TV crews move out?
Where's the feel
of a fresh sea breeze,
or the hiss
of surf through shingle?

brand.new*

They're designer labelling,
McDonaldising,
Coca-colonising the globe.
Well, I refuse to wear a label,
to be branded by the Beast,
worse than Cain because of Abel;
I'll only wear that New Name
on my forehead.
It's economic warfare now
waged by multi-nationals, with logos
better known than national flags.
I'll not pay the brand bullies
to advertise their products
on any part of my anatomy,
parasites that make their money
exploiting child labour
in their new colonies,
then make a second killing
exploiting their own young
by charging them to fit in.
They're stealing our culture,
commercialising our youth
from toddler on,
emasculating protest,
stifling creativity,
by dictating what is 'cool'.
They've branded a generation,
herded, brand-controlled;
subtly, made them bully each other
to pay the sucker premium
just to be cloned lookalikes,
to wear and advertise the mark.
No, I'll not wear their trainers,
eat their fast food,
accept their tainted grants,
or vote their puppet politicians in.

*Exhibition at the Victoria and Albert Museum 2000

War Memorial

This monument to youth spent
in sordid terror and confusion,
images of death and blood.
Meaningless flags are raised,
displaying the separations
and the motives
for a war over marks and lines
on a map
of ideologies,
continued
until the percentage in it fell
for distant politicians,
rivals for the title
of saviour of the world.

The Death's Lover*

Now, when you sing Death's Lover,
where's the romance
to tingle down your spine,
when high-tech wars
become video games,
leaving only black holes behind
and dead bodies
for edited TV highlights?

*Marching song of the Spanish foreign legion

Mary

Total 'Yes'
Total woman
Total joy
Total gift
to God

St Clare

"Little Plant" of Francis,
radiant in beauty
and holy joy,
you became
a clear spring
reflecting God's glory
as in a mirror.

You saw reality
with pure eyes;
following Christ
in poverty of spirit,
your life became,
in that clear light,
a mirror of the Gospel
to our world.

Mother Julian's Cell*

Odd to find you
in that industrial sprawl,
your cell
now in a modern church,
the same site
but more substantial
than your medieval hut.
Still one window on the world,
the other on the altar;
open to your neighbour, while
meditating on the Trinity
and its meaning, love.

A mystic
in the midst of life,
seeking God
amidst death, disease
and turmoil.
Revealing
hints and traces
of that other life,
that all will be well
and all manner of things
will be well –
even sin, somehow.

*Julian of Norwich

The Cloud of Unknowing

Slowing down,
tuning into God's time,
putting busyness on hold.
A solitary walk, a familiar path,
a heavy mist on a quiet sea;
light playing on the rippling waves,
its source I cannot see, but know.
Thoughts surface from the deep
and consciousness is stirred;
a lapse of time I cannot measure,
the gold of more than thought,
sharp darts of longing love
begin to rise to pierce the cloud.
Behind the parting mist the sun,
a faint and silver disc,
appears and fades.
Delight unbounded fills my heart,
not held by thought, but love.

Mary (2)

God came bodily
to one
who had already
received him spiritually,
in her heart
made room for him.
Then, come fill the void
in all our hearts
with the presence
of her Son;
may your will
be done in mine,
may Christ
be formed in me.

St Martin of Tours*

In midwinter
Martin, a solider
then eighteen,
cut his cloak in two,
gave half to a beggar
he saw naked
at the city gate.
Next night he had a dream:
Christ in his half cloak
said to the angels,
"Martin, still a catechumen,
wrapped me in this garment".

When the barbarians
were invading Gaul,
before battle,
he refused the Emperor's gift,
said it was wrong
for a soldier
of Christ to fight,
offered to stand unarmed
before the enemy line
under protection
solely of the Cross.
But Christ decided
he owed his soldier
no less a victory
than the enemy's submission.
Next day the enemy
sent delegates to sue for peace.

Becoming first a monk,
then bishop of Tours,
he did not cease to be a monk
but made himself a monastery
outside the city walls,
hollowed out the mountain rock.

Vowed to poverty,
the monks passed all gifts to the poor:
"We are fed by the Church
provided we seem to appropriate
nothing to ourselves".
A man of action
as well as meditation,
and famous for miraculous powers,
he was said to have raised the dead.

When he was praying in his cell,
the devil stood before him
clad as if in glory,
dressed as if a king,
asking Martin
to acknowledge him as Christ.
Martin replied that he refused
to believe that Christ had come
save in the state and form
in which he suffered,
save if he saw
the print of the nails:
at which the spirit vanished,
leaving behind an evil odour.

Past eighty,
when a fever was upon him.,
he lay dying,
wrapped in sackcloth,
laid in ashes.
He said
"Sons, it becomes
a Christian to die in ashes".
When the evil spirit
confronted Martin
on his deathbed,

Martin said:
"Why stand here?
You will find nothing in me
that belongs to you.
Abraham's bosom
is receiving me".
His face became transfigured,
becoming white as snow,
clothed now in the cloak
of his resurrection.

*316-397 AD

The Restless Heart

"You have made us for yourself, O Lord,
and our hearts are restless
until they rest in you."
St Augustine
Confessions

Restless searching,
seeking, longing,
aching for the One
we seek in every face
and thing,
but know not;
dissatisfied,
condemned
to infinite eternal longing,
dissatisfied with less,
dissatisfied with second best,
and always when we've found,
and grasped,
deluded.

Surrender to the One
the only answer,
surrender to that
crucible of fire
that consumes all other fires,
the death of self desire.
Swept up with holy longing,
to risk to open wide
to that transforming love,
to that tremendous Lover,
to imitate the Cross
in non-exclusive love
for all.

Healing Darkness*

Following
the way marked out
by God's will,
the dark way
of naked faith.
Nor this, nor that,
detached,
the way of nothing,
emptied of everything
but Him:
cast upon the All.

Suffering, searching;
desire for Him alone
awakened.
Longing to be
full of love,
filled with His love,
drawn into Him.
My 'Yes' repeated and repeated:
loving light, transforming fire,
living now in Him.

The swift-winged bird
at peace,
the soul unshackled.
Intimate converse
far beyond thought or word:
full of ardour,
touched by God.
Sure of Him,
loving 'Yes';
union of wills in love,
His will now done in mine.

*Spirituality of St John of the Cross

Epiphany

Where grey skies
meet the grey sea,
a small gap
where hope appears,
the golden sun
begins to flood the deep.

Even though
it's blackest black,
my God, inside,
deep down,
I love you
deepest deep.

Presence and Absence

If God is goodness,
truth and beauty,
and we are in his image
and reflect him,
then life is only bearable
if it's art,
otherwise can it be lived?
In the ugly, sordid, boring
and the everyday,
is God missing?
Does he come and go?
Is he there for only some?
Does he turn his head?
If life is what we make it,
why don't we all make it?
Suffered experience,
living life in monochrome,
in hazy black and white.

But it's when we're lost and empty,
then we grow; if we let him
God comes in to fill.
It's a mystery of freedom and grace.
When he seems most absent,
then he's present.
He brings light
to darkest dark.
We meet him in the now,
if we're really present
to the intensity of every day.
Joys that come unlooked for;
the past transformed,
interpreted by love.
But it's a deep abyss,
however thin the interface
between heaven and human space.

Call and Response

Through prayer,
and through the other,
the infinite Other
calls,
awakening response,
drawing me out
of self,
discovering truth
in the face-to-face
encounter,
going out to the Absolute
through the face
of the human
other.

A creature-in-relation,
self-risk undertaken,
radical compassion
in response to others' needs;
substituting for the other
in joyful
responsibility.
Forming my cross
in inevitable
insufficiency,
then, rooted in Christ,
encountering the power
of His transforming
love.

Poetry in Motion

Fingers still,
the pen poised
in suspense,
beyond thought,
the heart filled
with delight;
time stopped,
the senses frozen,
listening
to the least stir
of the imagination.
Creating
a sacred space,
seeing
what comes in.
Striving for words
to shape the ecstasy
of silent secret music,
of half-heard melodies
from afar;
reworking vague memories
and sad echoes;
the rest is observation.

Memory

Surely it's too early
for the leaves to fall?
Bare trees, for me,
send shadows of the lately dead
we had not loved enough.
I wanted still the summer sun,
the scent of flowers,
to remind me of your youth.

Those days seemed
so long,
days of sun and gladness,
endless sunny summer days.
Was there ever a dull one?
When did we ever plan
for rain?
When did they ever end?

What use is memory
now, when it's too late for joy?
Longing to share
what cannot now be shared.
Memories are sent to haunt
the quiet time by firelight.
Will only memory survive
the death of fire?

Death of a Poet

I muse in the evening air
amidst graveyard crosses set in rows.
A good deep grave
where lies a poet lately dead.

The world will miss your ready wit and charm.
There's no library with its stock of books
held more wealth of knowledge
than your wise old head.

With all your welcoming
of that sweet sister death,
where did the angels take you?
Is it far? How deep is the abyss?

And are there words
that once escaped your pen?
And does the Muse live there?
Mystic, enter then the mystery!

Now you know its secret,
sleep sound.

Walking with Philosophers

On his walks
Kierkegaard wore a top hat.
Kant was invariable,
doing exactly the same circuit
exactly on time.
Aristotle, too, was a bore
with his categories and specimen collecting.
To walk with Kafka was a trial
and one avoided Camus like the plague.
Heidegger was always accused
of never being on time.
Ockham was often scruffy,
having trouble with his razor.
Descartes' strides were pure extension,
and while Husserl's were phenomenal,
poor Empedocles' were fragmented.
Einstein was relatively sane;
but Wittgenstein
had a thing about pork pies
and a private language
no one understood.
Plato instead circled
in his winged chariot high above.

Zoo Life

All those creatures
caged and boxed,
confined in tanks,
made to live as narrowly
as we live,
exhibiting our neuroses
and psychoses,
anti-nature
classified as nature.

Perhaps we could
break loose
and go with one of them
to live as they do,
wild and free
of all of our possessions
and obsessions,
free to converse
with sea and air,
wind and rain,
and cool, running rivers.

But that's the foolish dream
of hothouse plants
that learn to thrive
in artificial climes,
condemned to glimpse
through a hazy fug
a freer world
outside.

Time Poor
(A 'rap')

Too busy to live:
on the treadmill 7 to 7,
stressed out, living
24/7.
Hop into the car:
traffic jam.
Shop till you drop:
choice fatigue.
Too much choice,
feeding dreams:
got to get that
something new.
Back at home:
TV, fast food,
channel-hopping.
Surf the Net:
no time to relate,
pass the time of day.
Don't stop to ask
what's life about.
Mod-cons, freeing
time for what?
Busy creating
stress on stress.
Progress to the abyss:
breaking point.
Too tired to sleep:
popping pills,
instant fix.
Party all night:
hours spent
chilling out.
What's this about
work-life balance?
What's it cost
to get back in touch
with the spiritual
self?

A Door Standing Open

A door standing open,
half closed, half open,
sunlight and shadow,
beckoning, challenging,
promising hope
of future joy,
but risk of sorrow
and a leave-taking,
a letting go.

A door I must pass through
to move from shadow
into full light of day,
a door standing open,
half closed, half open.
A door entered
and left behind,
or a door passed by?

Paradoxes

Silence can be the shortest
or the longest distance
between two people.
The distance
between two hearts
can be more than words can bridge.
Two hearts in love
can bridge any distance.
Love is beyond time and distance,
requires no words.
Time stops in love,
distance decreases;
but time creates distance
if there was never really love.

Silence

Communication
was total.
Our silence
was its fullness.
Our understanding
needed no words
to pass through
that infinite
zero point.

Fragments

"I cannot endure iniquity and
solemn assembly.
Your new moons and your pilgrim
feasts
my soul hates."   Isaiah 1:14

Will piety save
the unforgiving,
mere rites and sacrifices
cleanse those without compassion?
Is anger so durable
it masks the flight of birds?
Will our greed deprive us
of wilderness and peace?
Will love and hate be reconciled
in mercy's redeeming rain?

Eclipse of the Moon

Lady moon
is red tonight.
See, she weeps
red tears,
when her Sun's light
is blocked
by our sinful earth.
She is turned
blood red
by the shadow
of our blackness.

Why?

Why were we made
so fragile?
– For love and joy.
But why this risk
of suffering and pain?

And why this freedom?
– For good.
But why this risk of evil:
the sinner's guilt,
the victim's shame?
And why do children
suffer?

His Son the symbol
of guiltless suffering,
he risked
to make us free
to choose to love him;
he's there with us
in our suffering.

Hosea

The Father
holds us cheek to cheek,
stoops down to lift us up,
leads us with reins of kindness
with leading-strings of love.
His heart recoils from giving rein
to his fierce anger.

He lures us
out into the desert
to betroth us,
to speak into our hearts;
he wants us back,
wants us as lovers,
to prepare us
to meet him face to face.

The Lamb of God

To let go
of this... and this...
and all
that drags us down
and keeps us chained
and bound.
To open fully
to the sacrificial Lamb.
To believe that
in his loving mercy
he HAS
taken all our sin
because he loved us
while we were sinners still.
There is nothing he did not
die for, give his life for;
to believe it confidently
and firmly,
now in our sin we are
set free
of this... and this...
If we ask forgiveness
we have it now –
life, healing for the hidden,
wounded self.
For every moment
that we grasp it,
his life
infused within us;
even now eternal life,
true life, true love,
true beauty and communion
with each other.

If we give in instead to him,
if we let go of this... and this...,
allow him
to lift us up
to live the Christ life,
living with his life
within us
even now.

Crucified Love

Jesus came forward,
stood out of line
for my sake,
for all of us,
as the one who saves.
Entered the Jerusalem
of my heart,
bringing pain, bringing joy.
He came to heal
and to set free,
to open all things hidden,
out of darkness
bringing light.

Crucified love
darkened by my self-will,
misunderstood, abused
by my rejection
of his truth;
piercing his side,
God's heart broken,
tearing the veil,
breaking open
the well
of life-giving water,
revealing
the source of love for all.

If we too die –
die to sin –
and rise with him,
obedient, surrendered to love,

Christ crucified and risen
becomes for us the bridge
that spans the abyss
between fallen man
and man redeemed
and deified;
response to grace
the way to transformation
and salvation.

"I thirst"

His human heart
thirsty with
the Father's thirst
for us
to come to Him.

In that loud cry
upon the cross,
showing God's great desire
for us,
embodying our response.

Crucified Love (2)

You show yourself
to us
in the crucified
hands and feet
of those around us.
You ask us to serve
you in them,
not to take
but give,
to 'suffer with',
to share their hurt,
to bring your hope,
to share their joy.

Theo-Drama: The Artwork of God*

An encounter with
God's Beauty,
an act of love,
responding freely
to God's
self-emptying love;
dividing reality
from what is false
and evil,
giving witness,
to the point of death,
to truth.

The icon
of Christ's saving death,
holding a mirror
to life's drama,
providing a disclosure
of transcendent beauty,
showing what
we must do and suffer;
a stage erected
for the Christian,
as actor, not spectator,
called to act out
that creative,
self-surrendering
"Yes" of Christ
for all.

*The theology of Hans Urs von Balthasar

God's Beauty: Painting the Word

Something of that
heavenly beauty
beyond the senses,
something of that delight,
unbounded joy,
can penetrate the heart
when we reach out
in love to others.
When the imagination
is first stunned
by that transforming beauty
of Christ's teaching,
and his transfigured
sacrificial love,
drawing the soul
into communion
with God's glory,
set blazing in the heart
with ardent longing
for that image, almost lost,
of tender love and truth,
that haunting beauty stirs
and resonates within.

Faith

All seems black
and empty,
dark night of faith;
surrendered,
waiting for something deep
to shift within.
Does God exist
when the heart runs dry
and imagination fails?

At the level of faith,
beyond thought
and feeling,
there I find Him
gently prompting,
gently turning
and re-turning
love to love.

The Word

Above the din,
the sound and fury,
of many false
and empty words,
one Word
came forth
from silence,
a life-giving word
coming from the centre,
the still small voice
where all things
converge.

Eucharist

Bread broken,
wine poured out,
self-emptying,
endlessly
self-giving.

Share in the cup,
His will done,
a wide heart,
forgiving,
embracing all.

Make of us
your bread of life,
Christ's presence
nourishing
the world.

Easter Blossom

The ripe fruit
of the sacrifice
of blossom
that consents to fade.

The ripe fruit
containing the seed
that must die
to bring new life.

The ripe fruit
from the wood
of the tree
that brings new birth.

Spring

The robin singing
on a clean-cut stump
of tree,
from which young shoots
and budding leaves,
a curious red,
break forth.
Break my
hard heart, Lord,
and put a song
in me.

The Mystic Path

Golden sun,
the air ethereal,
liquid gold the water.
It was at the end of such a day,
walking in two worlds,
belonging to none,
I thought
I could
step out along
the golden highway
of the sea,
step across clouds
and reach the sun.